# The God Who Knows Me

## A Companion Devotional & Journal

**JOAN EMBOLA**

**THE GOD WHO KNOWS ME**

Copyright 2023 by Joan Embola

Love Qualified Press

All rights reserved.

No part of this book may be reproduced in any form or by any electronic or mechanical means, including information storage and retrieval systems, without written permission from the author, except for the use of brief quotations in a book review.

For more information, contact;

www.joanembola.co.uk

THIS BOOK BELONGS TO:

_____

__/__/__

# Also By Joan Embola

## Fiction
The One Who Knows Me: Sovereign Love Book 1
The One Who Loves Me: Sovereign Love Book 2
The One Who Sees Me: Sovereign Love Book 3
The One Who Holds Me: Sovereign Love Book 4

## Devotionals
Outpourings Of A Beloved Heart: A 30 Day Poetry Devotional About God's Love

*To my Heavenly Father, the God who knows me*

# INTRODUCTION

Dear beloved one,

Welcome to *The God Who Knows Me: A Companion Devotional & Journal*. Before you go into this book, I thought I'd tell you about the inspiration behind it and why I'm so excited for you to read it. After publishing my debut novel *The One Who Knows Me* in 2021, I realized the novel covered so many deep themes that would make good discussion topics and also journaling prompts. I've been journalling since 2014 and when God dropped this devotional idea in my heart, I thought it'd be cool to incorporate a space for journaling into it.

The devotional follows the main characters' journeys chapter by chapter and uses Bible passages to explore different aspects of God's sovereign love. If you've ever struggled with doubts about your faith in Jesus, then this book is for you. It tackles hard questions about how to deal with suffering, depression, anxiety, loss, and many more, as a Christian. Through it all, this book is for those looking to know God more by studying the Bible, praying, and journaling.

If you have not yet read *The One Who Knows Me*, it would be perfect to read it alongside this devotional. If you have already read *The One Who Knows Me*, you can still read this devotional and it would be perfect for discussion with friends, family or even in a book club. I encourage you to engage with each journaling prompt, study the Bible passages and use the prayer points as a gateway to communicate with your Heavenly Father. My prayer is that our good Lord speaks to you and reveals His love to you in ways you have never experienced before. In Jesus' name. Amen.

*"For He knows the way that I take. When He has tested me; I will come forth as gold."*

*-Job 23:10*

# CHAPTER 1

## Scripture: Psalm 27:1-5

In this chapter, we meet our first main character, Teeyana Joy Sparks, and we quickly learn that she has been living in fear for a long time. She and her best friend Amara are victims of bullying and Teeyana is so driven by fear that she has allowed it to affect her sense of security. When she comes face to face with her bully, Olivia Hastings, she doesn't have the courage to do anything but run. The sad thing about this is that Teeyana doesn't run to God, but she runs away from Him. Through her internal monologue, we can decipher that Teeyana feels weak and has been relying on her own strength. We also see her becoming frustrated that she has not been able to redeem herself so far. Even when Amara tries to reassure her by pointing her back to a solution in God, Teeyana brushes that off quickly.

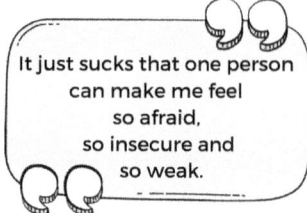

It just sucks that one person can make me feel so afraid, so insecure and so weak.

In Psalm 27, we see King David taking an opposite approach in the way he handles fear. Instead of running away from God like Teeyana, David runs to God and acknowledges the fact that He is the source of his security. David boldly declares that even though the wicked advance against him, or an army besieges him, or war breaks out against him, he will remain confident in who God is and what God can do.

Beloved one, as you go through today, remember that when you are deeply rooted in God, there will be no place for fear. The opposite of fear is faith and I'm not talking about faith in yourself or other human beings, but faith in God. The same God in whom David had so much confidence is the same God you serve today. He loves you.

## Journaling Prompt

*How do you respond in fearful situations?  
Do you run to or away from God?*

---

**Prayer:**
Dear Jesus, please help me to always run to you when I feel afraid.

**Today's affirmation:**
God is the strength of my life. I will not be afraid

# CHAPTER 2

## *Scripture: Exodus 16:1-12*

In this chapter, we see Teeyana spending a significant portion of it thinking about her past glory. She harbors so much anger inside of her because she longs for the old days when things were going well for her and her family. On the mountain of her life, her dad had a good job, they lived in a comfortable house in L.A, and she had friends in school who she got along with. But along the way, they reach a valley and her dad loses his job. They have to move to live with her grandparents, and she starts a new school where she is bullied. The interesting thing here is that it seems the only reason Teeyana believed in God before was because things were going well for her. She was more content with the life she was living, but not with the God who was sustaining her.

Back in L.A, my life was perfect. Dad had a good job, we had a cool house, Olivia didn't exist to me, and I had no doubts about God.

We see a similar pattern of behavior in Exodus 16:1-11. Two months had passed since the Israelites left Egypt. They were tired, exhausted and nowhere close to the Promised Land. So, like Teeyana, they turned to Moses and grumbled. They looked back and wished they were still in Egypt because in Egypt they had pots of meat and they could eat all the food they wanted. They forgot that the God who was in Egypt with them was the same God who delivered them out and who was still with them in the desert.

Beloved one, as you go through today, remember that God will always be God, no matter what your season is. Going through a valley won't change God's love for you. So instead of doubting and grumbling, I implore you to trust God today. He is faithful. He loves you.

## Journaling Prompt

*Have you been through valleys? Did you long for the old days too?*

---

**Prayer:**
Dear Jesus, please help me not to doubt you or grumble when I'm going through a valley.

**Today's affirmation:**
Even in the valley, God is still faithful.

# CHAPTER 3

## *Scripture: Psalm 34:15-20*

In this chapter, we meet Jayden Williams, who is in a different place in his faith journey and he is also facing a different set of struggles. Unlike Teeyana, who is doing all she can to run away from God, Jayden acknowledges that God is real and able to provide comfort. The only problem is that he is struggling to be vulnerable about how he is truly feeling. Both he and his parents are dealing with grief, but because Jayden is selfless, he feels the need to suppress his feelings because he wants to stay strong for his parents. He wants to be the one who encourages others to help them heal, but he does all this at the expense of his own healing journey.

There's only so much strength I can fake in front of my parents when deep inside, my heart is still shattered.

In 1 Samuel 21, David was running away from Saul, who was trying to kill him. David thought he would find refuge in Gath, under King Achish, but he was wrong. He had to run away again, and he hid in a cave at Adullam. David wrote Psalm 34 when he was hiding in this cave with some men who were with him. Even though David's men feared for their lives, he encouraged them to praise God because he knew that whenever we cried out to the Lord of hosts; He heard. David also knew that God is near to those who are broken-hearted and He is able to deliver us from all our troubles.

Beloved one, as you go through today, tell Jesus what your anxieties are. He is a friend that sticks closer than a brother. A friend who knows you more than any other and a friend who understands. You can be vulnerable with God. Pour out your heart to Him and let Him heal you of everything that ails your heart. He loves you.

# Journaling Prompt

*Do you feel weary and heavy hearted? Tell God all about it today.*

___

**Prayer:**
Dear Jesus, please help me to learn how to be vulnerable with You today.

**Today's affirmation:**
I will cast all my anxieties on Jesus because He cares for me.

# CHAPTER 4

## *Scripture: Galatians 5:1-6*

In this chapter, we delve more into another reason Teeyana wants to run away from God. During her inner monologue, she reveals that she finds faith in Jesus to be restrictive. She compares her faith journey to a tree that is dancing under the influence of the wind. She says the branches have no freedom to grow, and she doesn't want to be under His influence anymore. That's why she is so eager to leave her parents and go off to college. She wants the freedom to do things her own way, and the freedom to do what she thinks is right.

> That's exactly how I've been feeling--like these trees bending helplessly under the influence of the wind. Except in my case, it's not the wind bending my branches. It's God. I don't want Him bending my branches anymore. I want them free to grow.

In Galatians chapter 5, Apostle Paul challenged this kind of thinking in the minds of the believers in Galatia. He reminded them about the fact that we can find freedom nowhere else but in Jesus because He died to save us from sin and death. He picked us up from the miry clay, shattered the chains that bound us to destruction, and He redeemed us and adopted us into His family. The world tries to make us slaves to our emotions and feelings, while disguising it as freedom. New age beliefs, so-called progressive Christianity, and modern day witchcraft are some examples of powers trying to lure us away from the true freedom we have in Christ. But for you who believe in Jesus Christ, your chains are gone and you have been set free.

So, beloved one, as you step out today, choose to stay at the feet of Jesus. He is the only One who holds the key to your freedom. You are free indeed because He loves you.

## Journaling Prompt

*Are there any chains in your life?
Commit them into God's able hands today.*

---

**Prayer:**
Dear Jesus, please break every chain in my life that wants to keep me bound to the world.

**Today's affirmation:**
In Christ, I have true freedom. I am no longer a slave

# CHAPTER 5

## *Scripture: John 15:1-8*

In this chapter, Teeyana's dad finally confronts her about some things they have noticed about her attitude toward God. Teeyana mentions here that she doesn't need God because she wants to do things her own way. She doesn't believe that she needs to rely on God to strengthen her or empower her to go after the dreams He has laid in her heart. She just wants to do things without God.

In John chapter 15, our Lord Jesus Christ taught about vines and branches. In this passage, He used this demonstration to show that we can do nothing without Him. Just like the branches have to rely on the vine to bear fruit, so we must remain in God to thrive in our Christian walk. He strengthens us; He keeps us, and He holds us up when our strength fails. When we try to do things without Him, we end up frustrated, anxious and disappointed because we quickly realize that God is our source, and no one can thrive without a source.

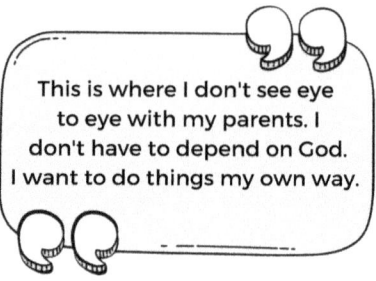

So, beloved one, as you go through today, remember that in God, you live and move and have your being. He is involved in every detail of your life, no matter how small it is. He sustains the universe, and He gives you the breath in your lungs. Depend on Him because He loves you.

# Journaling Prompt

*Are you struggling to depend on God?*
*Ask Him to show you how.*

___

**Prayer:**
Dear Jesus, help me to learn how to depend on You today.

**Today's affirmation:**
I am nothing without God. I will depend only on Him.

# CHAPTER 6

## *Scripture: 1 Chronicles 29:10-13*

In this chapter, we see Teeyana becoming vulnerable with Amara and she admits for the first time in the book that she is only good at putting up a show to make everyone believe she is in control of a situation. However, she still doesn't want to admit that God is in control. Teeyana already mentioned in the previous chapter that she struggles to accept the fact that she needs to depend on God to achieve her goals and dreams, so it makes sense that she also refuses to acknowledge His sovereignty.

In 1 Chronicles chapter 29, David made a prayer which has powerful declarations about the truth of God's sovereignty. This passage refers to God as the One who has greatness, power, glory, and majesty. It also declares that everything in heaven and earth belongs to Him. It says wealth and honor come from God and in His hands are strength and power. He is the ruler and head over all, therefore all glory and praise belong to Him.

> When we face challenges, I'm good at showing how in control I am—well at least until fear paralyzed me two months ago.

Beloved one, as you go through today, remember that while some may find the idea of God's sovereignty scary, the comfort you have is that this sovereign God is good, merciful and gracious. Refusing to acknowledge God's sovereignty doesn't change the fact that He is the one in the driver's seat. You didn't create yourself and you definitely didn't create the world we live in. So choose peace and comfort today by trusting in the One who did. He is always in control and He loves you.

## Journaling Prompt

*What area of your life are you struggling to surrender to God?*

_____
_____
_____
_____
_____
_____
_____
_____
_____
_____
_____
_____
_____
_____
_____

**Prayer:**
Dear Jesus, please help me to always be comforted by Your sovereign good hand over my life.

**Today's affirmation:**
God is always in control. I will put my trust in Him

# CHAPTER 7

## *Scripture: Psalm 139:1-12*

In this chapter, we see Teeyana finally in college, which is what she has been looking forward to. She is excited because she wants to make her own decisions and choose her own path. Despite her excitement to start afresh in college, she has repeatedly expressed that she feels alone on her journey. She feels nobody understands her doubts or her questions, so she continues to deal with everything on her own.

Sometimes, we too, like Teeyana, can adopt an orphan status and try to go through life without God's help because we think He won't understand. But when we do this, we are missing out on all the privileges we have as His children.

It's done now. I'm all on my own. All alone in New York City.

In Psalm 139, David talked about one of the wonderful characters of God, which is His omnipresence. He says in this passage that we can't go away from God's spirit because He is present everywhere—in the heavens, on the earth, beside us, behind us, ahead of us, and even in the darkness, His presence never leaves us. This is an incredibly comforting promise to hold on to as a child of God because it gives us the assurance that, even when we face hardships, God stays.

Beloved one, as you go through today, remember that when the world forsakes you, your family and friends leave you, God remains by your side. He is always near and always with you, so you are never alone. He loves you.

# Journaling Prompt

*Do you feel alone in your faith journey?
Tell God about it today.*

_____
_____
_____
_____
_____
_____
_____
_____
_____
_____
_____
_____
_____
_____
_____
_____
_____

**Prayer:**
Dear Jesus, thank You for always being by my side and never leaving me.

**Today's affirmation:**
God is always with me. I am not alone.

# CHAPTER 8

## *Scripture: 1 Kings 19:1-9*

IIn this chapter, we are in Jayden's point of view again and this time we see him engaging in an activity he believes to be a stress reliever. Even though playing basketball reminds Jayden of his brother—Tyler, he continues to do it because he has identified it as an effective way to help him stay distracted, so he can deal with the hurt that comes with his grief.

Life can get incredibly overwhelming sometimes and one thing that can be difficult for us to do is knowing when it's time to pause and rest. Unfortunately, we live in a world where people worship and glorify ambitions and productivity at the expense of looking after ourselves. This kind of lifestyle leads to burnout and burnout can affect our productivity, our physical and mental health.

> Basketball is such a stress reliever for me. And by stress, I mean all the pain in my heart that has refused to go away.

In the book of 1 Kings chapter 19, we see the prophet Elijah in a horrible place where he was feeling overwhelmed. He had received death threats from Jezebel, so he ran away because he feared for his safety. When he got to the wilderness, he was so depressed that he prayed for God to take his life because He had had enough. But when he fell asleep, the angel of the Lord appeared to him twice and encouraged him to eat and drink water. He was able to gain strength from the food so he could continue his journey.

Beloved one, as you go through today, acknowledge those moments when you feel overwhelmed. Take the necessary steps to rest, but ultimately go back to God to fill you up again. He will give you rest for your soul because He loves you.

# Journaling Prompt

*Do you feel stressed and anxious today?
Tell God all about it.*

_____
_____
_____
_____
_____
_____
_____
_____
_____
_____
_____
_____
_____
_____
_____
_____

**Prayer:**
Dear Jesus, please help me to learn how to rest in You.

**Today's affirmation:**
God is my rest. My refuge and strength is in Him.

# CHAPTER 9

## *Scripture: Psalm 43:1-5*

In this chapter, things take an interesting turn when Teeyana is thrust into another situation she has no control over. She was very excited about getting away from her parents and finally living on her own terms, but she never expected to have an unlikable roommate thrown into the mix. The main thing we see in this chapter is how Teeyana continuously refers to her experiences with bullying. Even though she is away from high school, her roommate situation takes her back to the time when she was bullied by Olivia Hastings.

> I've come too far to let anyone discourage me. Olivia might have gotten her way, but this red-haired girl won't.

While it is admirable that Teeyana tries not to allow herself to be discouraged, the problem, again, that we see here is that she tries to deal with it all on her own. When we haven't properly dealt with past traumas—whether emotional or physical—they affect the way we live our lives in the present. We clearly see this in Teeyana's case, where her situation with Olivia in the past makes her live in fear of what could be. We can't get ourselves out of difficult situations by trying to do it all on our own.

Beloved one, as you go through today, remember that God is able to heal you from the past traumas that are holding you back. So be encouraged to go back to Him today and ask Him to help you heal. He will help you because He loves you.

## Journaling Prompt

*Do you have any unresolved past trauma?
Tell God about them.*

_____

 

**Prayer:**
Dear Jesus, please help me heal from my past traumas.

**Today's affirmation:**
God is my hope and my healer.

# CHAPTER 10

## Scripture: 2 Corinthtians 12:9-10

In this chapter, we see Jayden's continuous struggle to be vulnerable about his past. He can't talk about his brother's death without breaking down, and he avoids talking about it as much as he can. It's not surprising that he is struggling with this because vulnerability is something that can be very hard to do. The reason this is hard is that it lays out your weaknesses in front of others and exposes you to criticism and judgement.

While being vulnerable is an important part of the healing process, if we are vulnerable to the wrong people, it can make matters worse. Being part of friendships and communities of people we can trust is helpful, as they can minister to us and encourage us.

To everyone else it's just a ribbon...but to me, it's a daily challenge to learn how to share my story with others.

But the best person we can be vulnerable with is with God.

Beloved one, as you go through today, remember that God understands what it means to go through suffering. He went through that for you on the cross of calvary. He understands your hurts, and He knows exactly how you feel. He can provide the strength you need in your moments of weakness because He is your source of strength. So go to God today and tell him how you feel. His grace is sufficient for you. He loves you.

## Journaling Prompt

*Do you have anything burdening your heart today? Be vulnerable with God and tell Him.*

_____
_____
_____
_____
_____
_____
_____
_____
_____
_____
_____
_____
_____
_____
_____
_____
_____

**Prayer:**
Dear Jesus, please help me draw strength from You when I am weak.

**Today's affirmation:**
When I am weak, God is strong. His grace is sufficient for me.

# CHAPTER 11

## *Scripture: Colossians 1:15-20*

In this chapter, we see Teeyana building her friendship with Jayden and she also has her first row with her roommate, Heather. When she tries to make peace with Heather, it doesn't go well, so Teeyana becomes frustrated and asks God a lot of questions. One question she asks is why things can't always go the way she wants them to. The simple answer to that is the fact that we are not sovereign.

Have you ever wondered what your life would be like if everything worked out the way you want? You would think that everything would be perfect for you, but what about how your actions impact the lives of others, the connections you make, the people you meet, and the relationships you build? Can you also control all those things?

I just want to have it all under control in my own world. Is that too much to ask?

The more you think about this, the more you'd realize that God's sovereignty goes beyond ourselves. He doesn't just hold your life together, but He holds the lives of your family, your friends, your loved ones and all people all around the world. Our view of life is restricted, but God sees everything. He holds the past, present and future together and the wisdom in which He rules us all is great and no one can understand it. Life is unpredictable and sometimes God can place you in a situation that pushes you out of our comfort zone for your own good.

So, beloved one, commit that uncomfortable situation into God's hands and pray that He teaches you to trust in Him and act in accordance to His sovereign will over your life. He loves you.

## Journaling Prompt

*Are you in an uncomfortable situation? Tell God about it today.*

---
---
---
---
---
---
---
---
---
---
---
---
---
---
---
---
---
---
---
---

**Prayer:**
Dear Jesus, give me wisdom to act in accordance to your will when I'm in uncomfortable situations

**Today's affirmation:**
God is sovereign and good. I will trust in Him.

# CHAPTER 12

## *Scripture: Romans 5:1-11*

In this chapter, we see Teeyana having her first conversation with Jayden about God. Initially, she doesn't want to reveal that she is from a Christian home, but when Jayden finds out, he is thrilled—a reaction Teeyana didn't expect because she sees nothing special about being a child of God. She sees no big deal about being loved by the God who created the universe and the God who has all the power. In her mind, Teeyana chastises Jayden for his belief in God and accuses him of taking his faith too seriously.

But is there ever such a thing as taking God too seriously? The seriousness with which we take our walk with God equates to the serious thing Jesus did for us at the cross of Calvary. While it is very easy for people to take God's grace for granted by making a mockery of it, or accusing us of being foolish, we who believe know better. Jesus dying on the cross, saving us from our sins, and snatching us away from darkness into light, was serious business. That act alone brought us salvation from eternal death. It wiped all our sins away, and it spared us from the wrath of God, which we so rightly deserve.

The problem is that he takes this God thing way too seriously and I don't.

Now we live our lives for God's glory alone because we are new creatures filled with never ending joy, hope and peace that surpasses all human understanding. Jesus is our reason for living, our reason for breathing, and our reason for waking up every morning. He is coming back again some day to take us away from this cruel world, so we can spend eternity in the fullness of His glory. So, beloved one, if you have been taking advantage of God's grace, I encourage you to go back to your first love and pursue a deeper connection with Him today. He loves you.

## Journaling Prompt

*Have you ever taken advantage of God's grace? How can you remedy that today?*

_____
_____
_____
_____
_____
_____
_____
_____
_____
_____
_____
_____
_____
_____
_____
_____
_____

**Prayer:**
Dear Jesus, please help me to always cherish your gift of salvation.

**Today's affirmation:**
God is my Savior. I will forever be grateful to Him.

# CHAPTER 13

### *Scripture: 2 Corinthians 10:1-5*

In this chapter, Teeyana's story takes another interesting turn where we see her battling with peer pressure. This is a girl who has craved to do whatever she wants for so long, and when an opportunity presents itself, she makes the conscious decision to follow her feelings and emotions instead of doing what is right. The consequences of Teeyana's actions are realized quickly in this scenario, but this is not always the case as some people might only experience consequences much later when a lot of damage has already been done.

Just one glass, Teeyana. You want to fit in, here's your chance.

Everyone wants to be loved and to have that sense of belonging and acceptance. But the problem with this is that if we're not relying on God, we can find ourselves desperately trying to fit in with the wrong crowd of people, whose friendships will draw us away from Him.

In 2 Corinthians 10, the Apostle Paul talks about the fact that Christians whose hearts have been transformed by the gospel of Jesus Christ do not live according to the world's standards. The pressure to follow what society says is at its peak, but as children of God, we know that God's Word is our standard and our final authority.

Beloved one, the company you keep could make or break you, so it's important that you surround yourself with people who care about your spiritual health—not people who will pressure you to compromise your values and convictions. You can rely on God to help you find this type of community. He loves you.

# Journaling Prompt

*Are you struggling with peer pressure?
Ask God to help you find godly friends.*

___

**Prayer:**
Dear Jesus, please help me to choose friends that will encourage me in my walk with You.

**Today's affirmation:**
I will rely on God to help me choose godly friends.

# CHAPTER 14

## *Scripture: 1 Corinthians 13:1-7*

In this chapter, we see Jayden taking a different approach to his life by following the Holy Spirit's leading. He seeks godly and wise counsel in order to encourage his new friend Teeyana. He wants to help her, but he doesn't know how to go about it, so he asks Anton and Annie for help. They remind him that God can use him as a tool and they encourage him to never stop praying about the situation.

It can be very discouraging when you pray for someone to come to the knowledge of Christ and time passes without you seeing any results. In this chapter, one important thing Anton and Annie point out is that God is the one who changes hearts.

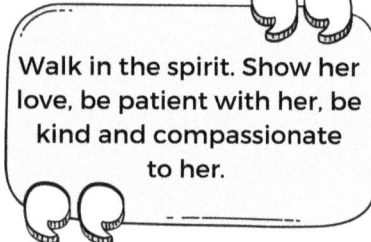

Walk in the spirit. Show her love, be patient with her, be kind and compassionate to her.

Our own part is to show God's love, not just to our brothers and sisters in Christ, but also to those who do not know God.

In 1 Corinthians 13, we see that love is an action and if we cannot love others, then we can't say that we truly love God. The foundation of the gospel is the love of God and our Savior, Jesus, is the embodiment of God's love for us. The Bible encourages us to love each other genuinely because this is the greatest way we can witness to others about Christ. It is not an easy thing to love others. That is why we need to rely on the Holy Spirit for help to take away any pride that prevents us from doing this.

So, beloved one, as you step out today, purpose it in your heart to love others and ask God to help you. He loves you.

# Journaling Prompt

*Do you struggle to love others?*
*Ask God for help today.*

___

**Prayer:**
Dear Jesus, please help me to love others the way You want me to.

**Today's affirmation:**
God is love. He loves me so I will love others too.

# CHAPTER 15

## *Scripture: Galatians 6:1-10*

In this chapter, we see Teeyana dealing with her first hangover and how Jayden swoops in and helps her through it. It is a good follow up from the previous chapter where Jayden asked for help on how to encourage Teeyana. The advice he got was to show her love, and love is kind, so Jayden chooses to be kind to Teeyana. Jayden's reaction surprises Teeyana because she was expecting him to rain down judgemental comments on her, but this is not the case.

> This was not the reaction I was expecting to get from him. Why is he so nice to me?

Have you ever met someone who has left the church? One common reason they mention is that they were hurt by the church. Many people give accounts of being abused, insulted, condemned, shunned, and these actions made them leave. It is sad to hear such accounts because God's children should be able to look out for each other.

It is important for us to hold each other accountable, and that includes calling out our sins and encouraging each other back to God. But the Bible also teaches us to do this gently, humbly, and in love. If there is no love, then we are not doing it in the name of God.

So, beloved one, if you have been burned by Christians and are struggling to go back to the community of believers, God can heal your heart and strengthen your relationship with Him today. He loves you.

# Journaling Prompt

*Have you been hurt by the church?*
*Tell God about it today.*

_____
_____
_____
_____
_____
_____
_____
_____
_____
_____
_____
_____
_____
_____
_____
_____
_____
_____
_____
_____

**Prayer:**
Dear Jesus, please heal me completely from anyone who has hurt me in the church.

**Today's affirmation:**
God is able to heal my hurt. I will trust Him.

# CHAPTER 16

## *Scripture: Ephesians 1:3-14*

In this chapter, we see Jayden celebrating Teeyana's acceptance to come to the youth group social. To Teeyana, her saying yes is just a way of not repeating her previous mistake of giving in to peer pressure and doing something she doesn't want to do. But to Jayden, Teeyana saying yes is an answered prayer. One important thing to note here is that Jayden acknowledges the fact that God was the one who worked on Teeyana's heart and brought about the change.

It was only a little step. She had not yet fully surrendered to God, but Jayden was thankful and in that moment of victory, he remembered to give thanks to God.

> I think her heart is softening and I have only God to thank for that.

When we are praying for people to come to the knowledge of God, it can be disheartening when nothing seems to change. But we often forget that all we are doing is planting seeds. The Holy Spirit then goes ahead to water it and bring about the increase we want to see. How long it takes is entirely up to God and it may never even be in our lifetime. But our hope lies in the fact that God is always working. Even when we don't see any progress or any growth or it feels our prayers are useless, God is still working. God draws us to Him and He is the one who opens our eyes to see the treasure that is in Him. God is responsible for turning our heart of stone into a heart of flesh and He alone makes us willing to serve and obey Him.

So, beloved one, as you go through today, remember that your part in this world is to share the gospel and leave the rest to God. He knows what He is doing and He will do just what is right. He loves you.

# Journaling Prompt

*Are you praying for someone to know Jesus?
Commit them into God's hands today.*

_____
_____
_____
_____
_____
_____
_____
_____
_____
_____
_____
_____
_____
_____
_____
_____

**Prayer:**
Dear Jesus, help me to trust and take comfort in Your sovereignty over our salvation.

**Today's affirmation:**
God is sovereign over salvation. I trust in His good and perfect ways.

# CHAPTER 17

## *Scripture: Job 1:1-20*

In this chapter, we see Teeyana having a conversation with Heather. So far, the story has not shown Heather in a good light, but Heather asks a very valid question which stuns Teeyana. Why do we believe in God? What is the basis of our faith in Jesus? Is it because we have money, a roof over our head, or a functional family? Do we believe because God has always answered our prayers? What if all of that was stripped away? Would we still have faith in God then?

In the story of Job, the Bible tells us that Satan believed the only reason Job was upright in his ways was because God had blessed him with a big family, many servants, livestock, etc. He was so sure that if God stripped Job of everything he owned, Job will cave in and curse God.

> **Would you still believe in God if things weren't working for you?**

But we can see when we read the passage till the end, that even in the midst of all that turmoil (and it was a lot of turmoil), Job refused to curse God and he didn't charge God with any wrongdoing. Can you also boldly proclaim that for yourself? Does the measure of your faith depend on whether you have plenty or in need? Is it easier to trust God when everything is going right than when things are seemingly going wrong?

Beloved one, I implore you to lean on God today no matter what your situation is. The God who soars with you on the mountain is the same God who walks beside you in the valley. That's why the Apostle Paul was able to boldly proclaim in Philippians 4:13 that he can do all things through Christ who strengthens him. So whether you are on the mountain or the valley, put your faith in God. He has nothing but good thoughts for you. He loves you.

## Journaling Prompt

*Do you struggle to be content when you are in the valley? Tell God about it today.*

___

**Prayer:**
Dear Jesus, give me faith to trust You even when I'm going through the valleys of life.

**Today's affirmation:**
I will always be content no matter what my situation is.

# CHAPTER 18

## *Scripture: Romans 8:28-30*

In this chapter, we see Teeyana opening up and talking about her feelings again. She unpacks all her emotions and pours her heart out to Jayden, because she wants to understand why he is so confident in God. She is envious that he seems to have it all together and she is not only looking for someone to validate her feelings, but also someone to give her the answers she desperately seeks. Jayden uses this opportunity to encourage her, as he has always wanted to do.

One thing he tells her is that in order for us to experience the goodness of God's character, we need to be in a position where we can't rely on anyone else but God. We can't know God to be our

> If we never have any problems, then we would never know that God is a problem solver.

provider if we have not been in need. We can't experience God as our healer, if we have nothing to be healed from. We can't experience God as our Savior if we have not found ourselves in the deep end, fighting to keep our head above the water. God is intentional in the way He has planned our lives. Nothing takes Him by surprise. The events of our lives are all part of one big puzzle, but our view is limited and only God can see the big picture.

So, beloved one, if you are stuck in a particular season of your life today, asking God all those questions and trying to understand, I implore you to ask God to allow you to experience the goodness of His character in that situation. Because of Him, your life is still worth living, even if it doesn't make sense. He loves you.

## Journaling Prompt

*Are you struggling to make sense of your life right now? Tell God about it today.*

_____
_____
_____
_____
_____
_____
_____
_____
_____
_____
_____
_____
_____
_____
_____
_____
_____
_____
_____

**Prayer:**
Dear Jesus, thank You for making my life worth living.

**Today's affirmation:**
There's no pain without a purpose. God is always intentional.

# CHAPTER 19

## *Scripture: Acts 11:19-26*

In this chapter, we see Teeyana and Amara back home in Boston for Christmas break and they are sharing their college experiences. During their conversation, Amara notices that because Teeyana has been spending a lot of time with Jayden, her outlook on life has changed. Teeyana has become more hopeful about seeing the good in others—including her roommate—Heather.

I'm just realizing that the world is not only full of bad people after all.

This shows how important it is to be around the right people and the right friends, who will encourage us when the trials of life beat us down. In Acts chapter 11, the Bible explains that some Christians were scattered, and the church suffered persecution after Stephen was killed. So when Barnabas heard about this, he left Jerusalem and went to Antioch. While in Antioch, he encouraged all the believers there to keep following Jesus, despite what they were going through. Because of this encouragement, many people surrendered their lives to Jesus, too.

Beloved one, as you step out today, remember that there is so much persecution and opposition toward the church these last days. A discouraged and beaten down church can do nothing to witness to others. So, be around people who can encourage you when the going gets tough. Also, be intentional about encouraging others to follow Jesus, too. He loves you.

# Journaling Prompt

*In what way has God used the people around you to encourage you?*

_____
_____
_____
_____
_____
_____
_____
_____
_____
_____
_____
_____
_____
_____
_____
_____

**Prayer:**
Dear Jesus, thank You for putting people around me who encourage me.

**Today's affirmation:**
I will be a blessing and encouragement to others.

# CHAPTER 20

## *Scripture: Psalm 73:21-26*

In this chapter, we see Teeyana expecting to receive bad news. Crippling anxiety takes over her, her emotions are all over the place, and the fear of loss paralyzes her. The intensity of it overwhelms her so much that Amara has to step in to encourage her before she can face whatever is waiting for her.

The prospect of anticipating bad news can be so nerve-wracking that our whole body shuts down. The physical symptoms of anxiety can include chest tightness, chest pain, palpitations, pins and needles sensation, dizziness, tremors, sweating, and even loss of consciousness. In those moments when our body fails us and we can't control how wild our thoughts run, there is one hope we have—Jesus Christ.

After everything that has happened in my family, I don't think my heart is strong enough to bear another piece of bad news.

Asaph, the author of Psalm 73, acknowledged in this Psalm that our hearts and our flesh may sometimes fail us, but even in those moments, it is not the end. Because God still lives and He will forever remain our strength and portion.

Beloved one, as you step out today, remember that God is your inheritance and your hope. So you can be joyful in the face of anxiety because its knees will eventually bow in the presence of Jesus, who is the keeper of your peace. He loves you.

## Journaling Prompt

*Are you feeling anxious about your flesh failing you? Tell God about it.*

---

**Prayer:**
Dear Jesus, thank You for always being my strength and my portion even when my flesh fails.

**Today's affirmation:**
God is my strength and my portion forever.

# CHAPTER 21

## *Scripture: 1 Kings 18:20-40*

In this chapter, we see Teeyana trying to make sense of the events of her life. She got to a point where she was starting to believe in God's goodness again. But now her life has taken a turn for the worse, so she turns to God and speaks to him for the first time in the book. But what she says proves she doesn't even know the God she serves. Her prayer is based on what other people have said to her about God and not what she believes Him to be.

When trials and tribulations come, do you pray to God because you truly believe that the promises in His Word are ye and amen, or do you pray to Him because that's what you were taught to do?

I know everyone says You are good so please, if that is true, let Grandma survive this

In 1 Kings chapter 18, the prophets of Baal wanted to prove that their god was alive. They spent hours crying and cutting themselves, but Baal did not answer. When Elijah finally cried out to God, He knew He served a God who could do all things. So he pleaded for God to prove Himself and He did. This story emphasizes the mighty power of God and this reminder is important to renew our minds when we face trials. We are so often driven by fear of what we can see that we forget we serve a God who is omnipotent.

Beloved one, instead of cowering amid trials today, tell the troubles how big your God is and then call on the name of your God—who you believe is able to do exceedingly more than you can ever ask or think. He loves you.

## Journaling Prompt

*Are you going through trying times?
Call upon God today.*

---

**Prayer:**
Dear Jesus, thank You for always answering me when I call on You.

**Today's affirmation:**
God is bigger than my trials. I will always call on Him.

# CHAPTER 22

## *Scripture: Mark 14: 32-41*

In this chapter, we see Teeyana continuing to grapple with the tragedy that has befallen her family. She struggles with all the questions she had before about God and no matter how much she battles with herself, she still doesn't know how to find the answers. As her grandpa leads them in prayer, Teeyana is offended that he prays for God's will and she asks about what God's will is in the situation they are in. She wonders whether God will let her grandma live or die.

In Mark 14, we see our Lord Jesus preparing for his crucifixion by staying in the place of prayer. At the garden of Gethsemane, He prayed fervently by first acknowledging that there is nothing

**What is God's will in this situation? Is He going to heal her? Or is He going to let her die?**

God cannot do. Then He asks God to take away the cup of suffering from Him, but He also said above all, let God's will be done and not His. In that moment, Jesus knew that God's will is infinitely more good and worthy of submitting to.

Do you pray for God's will in your life? Or are you afraid that His will will not be what you want? God's ways are not yours. His will toward you is good and perfect, even if it doesn't align with your desires. So praying for God's will means praying that your desires align with His desires and that your mind can be renewed so that you can appreciate His will for what it truly is—good and perfect.

So, beloved one, as you step out today, ask God to show you His will today. But above all, ask God to help you love His will. He loves you.

## Journaling Prompt

*Are you struggling to figure out what God's will is? Ask Him for clarity.*

---

**Prayer:**
Dear Jesus, please help me discern and love Your will for my life.

**Today's affirmation:**
God's will for me is good and perfect.

# CHAPTER 23

### *Scripture: Isaiah 43:1-7*

In this chapter, Jayden tries to encourage Teeyana by reminding her that God is with her and won't abandon her. He also prays for her and asks God to help her as she waits to hear the news about the outcome of her grandma's scans. In that moment, when Teeyana is encapsulated by the fear of the unknown, Jayden reminds her about an important attribute of God. He doesn't leave us alone in the rough waters.

Isaiah 43 holds comforting promises about those who put their trust in the Lord. It says that when we go through deep waters, God will be with us.

**God won't abandon you in the rough waters.**

When we go through rivers of difficulty, we will not drown. When we go through the fire of oppression, we will not be burned up and the flames will not consume us. I love the last part of verse 7 where God says that for those who have claimed Him as their God, He will bring them together from wherever they have been scattered to. For He has created us for His glory and we are His to keep.

Beloved one, if you are feeling discouraged today because of the deep waters, I encourage you to hold on to God's promises right now. He will never abandon you and He will never leave you. Continue to lean on Him through these trials as He leads you safely to your expected end. He loves you.

# Journaling Prompt

*Are you going through rough waters right now? Tell God about it.*

_____
_____
_____
_____
_____
_____
_____
_____
_____
_____
_____
_____
_____
_____
_____
_____
_____
_____

**Prayer:**
Dear Jesus, help me to lean on You alone when I go through the rough waters.

**Today's affirmation:**
God is with me through the rough waters. I never walk alone.

# CHAPTER 24

### *Scripture: Ruth 1:1-22*

In this chapter, we see Teeyana dealing with her worst fear. She actually prays to God and asks Him to let her grandma live, but the answer she gets is not what she wants. So she retreats into a black hole of sadness, believing with all her might that God has disappointed her.

It's one thing for humans to disappoint us because we know no one is perfect. But have you ever felt like God has disappointed you because He didn't answer your prayer or because your life didn't turn out the way you wanted? The story of Naomi, Ruth's mother-in-law, describes this kind of scenario. God had blessed  Naomi with a husband and children and daughters-in-law. But in the blink of an eye, almost everyone she loved died. When she returned to her homeland, she had let her disappointment consume her so much that she even asked people to call her Mara, which means bitter.

Disappointment is painful, confusing and can shake our faith in so many ways. But the truth remains that we must learn to cling to God to help us overcome it. The negative way to deal with disappointment is to turn away from God, but we can do absolutely nothing without Him. It is important to be honest with God about our feelings because He cares about them. But ultimately, we must ask God to help us cling to Him so He can help us heal and let go of the pain in our hearts.

Beloved one, remember that God can bring about redemption and salvation, just like He did with Naomi and Ruth. So bring all your disappointments to Him today. He will heal you because He loves you.

# Journaling Prompt

*Do you feel God has disappointed you?*
*Tell Him about it today.*

_____
_____
_____
_____
_____
_____
_____
_____
_____
_____
_____
_____
_____
_____
_____
_____
_____
_____

**Prayer:**
Dear Jesus, help me not to cling to You when I'm dealing with disappointment.

**Today's affirmation:**
God will heal me from the pain of disappointment. I choose to cling to Him.

# CHAPTER 25

## *Scripture: Lamentations 3:22-26*

In this chapter, Teeyana continues to process her emotions as she lives through all her worst fears of going through her grandma's funeral while still trying to believe she has everything under control. The pain eats at her heart and without knowing what to do with it all; she turns it into anger, which she directs at God.

Have you ever just felt like giving up when you look at the circumstances in your life or when you examine the state of the world right now? Have you ever felt like throwing in the towel because you have been praying for something, yet the situation keeps getting worse?

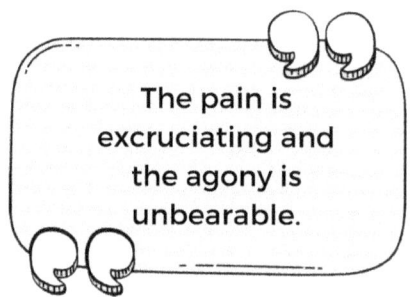

**The pain is excruciating and the agony is unbearable.**

In the book of Lamentations, we see an anonymous author lamenting and reflecting on the Babylonian siege of Jerusalem and the destruction and exile that followed. This book looks at the pain and confusion the Israelites went through as they dealt with the aftermath of that event. Reading about all the pain and suffering in this book can be depressing. However, amid all that lamenting, there are a few verses that remind us about why we can put our hope in God, even when there seems to be no way out. Verses 22-36 remind us about the fact that because God loves us, He will not abandon us to suffer forever. Weeping may endure for a night, but God is still the bringer of joy in the morning.

So, beloved one, as you go through today, remember that God is faithful to keep His promises. Don't give up. Continue to put your hope in Him. He loves you.

## Journaling Prompt

*Do you feel like giving up right now?
Tell God all about it.*

_____
_____
_____
_____
_____
_____
_____
_____
_____
_____
_____
_____
_____
_____
_____
_____
_____

**Prayer:**
Dear Jesus, help me to keep pressing on and never to give up.

**Today's affirmation:**
God will never cast me off forever. I will not give up.

# CHAPTER 26

## *Scripture: 1 Samuel 17:20-50*

In this chapter, we unravel one important foundation of Teeyana's doubts and that is her not knowing God. She doesn't know that He is the forgiver of sins and the One who is mighty to save. She also doesn't know that when God makes His promises, He doesn't go back on them. All she believes at this point in her life is that God can't help her, so she tries to seek answers to all her questions on her own.

Have you ever found yourself in a situation where you believed something about God but then found out it is not His character? Did you go to God to find out the truth, or did you try to look within yourself?

Whatever it is I've done, God hasn't forgiven me for it.

Sometimes, when people refer to the story of David and Goliath, they praise David's strength and bravery. But actually, the only reason David could defeat Goliath was because He knew the God He served. Just before the fight, David boldly told Goliath that his strength was not in his armor, but in the Almighty God whom He believed to be the God of the armies of Israel. David, even at his young age, had experienced God as a deliverer. The foundation for His confidence was, therefore, the character of God and not his own strength.

Beloved one, do you know God for yourself? It's easy to believe what other people say about God, what your pastor says, or what your parents say, or what your favorite Christian influencer says. But who is God to you? Resolve in your heart today that you will seek to know and experience God for yourself. It's the only way to stay rooted in Him when the trials of life come. He loves you.

## Journaling Prompt

*Do you know God?*
*Who is He to you?*

_____
_____
_____
_____
_____
_____
_____
_____
_____
_____
_____
_____
_____
_____
_____
_____
_____
_____

**Prayer:**
Dear Jesus, please help me to know You and experience You for myself.

**Today's affirmation:**
God is my God. I will seek to know Him always.

# CHAPTER 27

### *Scripture: Psalm 136:1-26*

In this chapter, Jayden experiences sadness when he cannot encourage Teeyana when she is going through a difficult time. He blames himself and all the feelings he had when he lost his brother, Tyler, start coming back. His emotions overwhelm him so much that He struggles to hold on to God's goodness even though He believes it to be true.

While it is fine to allow ourselves to feel hurt, pain, anger and sadness, it is very dangerous to let our emotions consume us so much that it makes us believe God is not good even though our hearts believe that to be true.

I know You are good, but nothing about this feels good.

Beloved one, as you step out today, remember that it doesn't matter how you feel. God will always be good. Our emotions and feelings do not change God's character. God remains the same no matter what our emotions try to make us believe. So even if you are in a situation that makes you believe God is not good, preach the truth of His love and goodness again and again to yourself. He loves you.

## Journaling Prompt

*Have your emotions prevented you from seeing the goodness of God? Tell God about it.*

_____
_____
_____
_____
_____
_____
_____
_____
_____
_____
_____
_____
_____
_____
_____
_____
_____
_____

**Prayer:**
Dear Jesus, help me to experience your goodness even when I don't feel it.

**Today's affirmation:**
God is always good. No matter how I feel.

# CHAPTER 28

## *Scripture: Psalm 42:5-11*

In this chapter, we see Jayden at his lowest point as he struggles to stay encouraged after what transpired between him and Teeyana. He believes he has been living a lie and is not qualified to encourage anyone because he couldn't encourage Teeyana. He is so drenched in his emotions that he desperately seeks to find hope and a reason to keep going. His response to discouragement is that instead of running away from God, he runs to God. He seeks wise counsel from Anton, who tells him to ask God to fill him up with hope again.

> You can't run on empty. Go back to the place of intimacy with Jesus.

In Psalm 42, the author encourages himself by speaking truths to himself. He acknowledges he feels downcast and discouraged. But he also reminds himself that his hope is in God, therefore, he will continue to praise Him for who He is and not just what He has done.

God is our rock and our refuge. He is our safe place and our solitude. When we are going through trials and tribulations, He is the one who provides us comfort and lifts our head. He is our shadow, the One who protects us and builds a shield around us. He is our peace during a time of chaos and we need him to get through these tough times.

Beloved one, even as a follower of Jesus, you will encounter diverse trials at some point. But when they come, instead of running away, go back to the place of intimacy with Jesus. Stay at His feet and pray that He fills you up with his hope. He loves you.

## Journaling Prompt

*Do you feel downcast today? Ask God to feel you up with hope again.*

_____
_____
_____
_____
_____
_____
_____
_____
_____
_____
_____
_____
_____
_____
_____
_____
_____
_____

**Prayer:**
Dear Jesus, please fill me up with Your hope.

**Today's affirmation:**
God is my hope. I will not be downcast. I will not be discouraged.

# CHAPTER 29

## *Scripture: Jonah 1:1-16*

In this chapter, Teeyana opens up to Amara about how she is feeling. She tells Amara that she doesn't think the God thing is working for her. She also tells Amara about her disappointments and how she feels let down by God. But instead of getting validation for her feelings, Teeyana gets words of caution from Amara. Amara points out that Teeyana has been trying to put God into a box. Amara also points out that Teeyana won't find the answers she seeks if she keeps running away from God and shutting everyone out. Although this conversation doesn't bring about a full on change of heart, it plants the seed in Teeyana's heart that gives her a lot to think about.

The story of the prophet Jonah is a great example of how it is not possible to run away from God. Wherever we try to go, He is there. We forget He is omnipresent, and He is involved in every little detail of our lives. Whether or not you choose to cling to Him, He remains God. Whether or not you decide to ask Him for help, He will always be God.

Beloved one, God has all the answers you seek, so when confusion comes, please don't run away from Him. Press in deeper, remain at his feet. He will give you the answers you need and even when He is silent, He will give you strength to endure. He loves you.

## Journaling Prompt

*Have you tried to run away from God?
Ask Him to draw your heart back to Him.*

_____
_____
_____
_____
_____
_____
_____
_____
_____
_____
_____
_____
_____
_____
_____
_____
_____
_____

**Prayer:**
Dear Jesus, draw me nearer and closer to You always.

**Today's affirmation:**
God is the answer. I will draw closer to Him always.

# CHAPTER 30

## Scripture: Exodus 4:1-17

In this chapter, we see Teeyana stumbling through the path in front of her because she has so many doubts. Even though she hoped to get the Google internship, when she finally gets the opportunity, she chooses to believe her doubts. She questions everything again, wondering whether she will succeed and also doubting everything she has been working hard for. We can see here that she gives in to her doubts so easily because the foundation of her belief is not strong enough. She is not confident in the path she is taking and therefore, she can't choose to hold on when the going gets tough. So instead of trusting God, she gives excuses.

What if I mess this up? What if I throw it all down the drain?

When God called Moses to go to Egypt to free the Israelites from slavery, he also had a lot of excuses to give to God. He didn't understand God's power and majesty, so he gave excuses because he had doubts. But God had to remind Moses of who He was and why He was sending him. It had nothing to do with Moses's abilities and everything to do with God's power. Doubts will always come, but if we put our trust in Jesus, we will have no reason to doubt. God never fails. He never changes. He is who says He is. His power is beyond measure.

Beloved one, if you are in a place of doubt at the moment where, like Moses, you are struggling to obey God's direction; I implore you to surrender to Him. There is no better reward than that which comes from serving God. He loves you.

# Journaling Prompt

*Have you been doubting God's plan for you? Pray for wisdom to obey.*

_____
_____
_____
_____
_____
_____
_____
_____
_____
_____
_____
_____
_____
_____
_____
_____
_____

**Prayer:**
Dear Jesus, please give me wisdom and help me to trust the path You have laid out for me.

**Today's affirmation:**
God knows what He is doing. I will trust Him.

# CHAPTER 31

### *Scripture: Genesis 22:1-19*

In this chapter, we see Jayden on his healing journey and he shares everything he has learned along the way. One of the important lessons he shares is that he needs to accept that he is not God. He misses Teeyana and wants to be in her life, but he knows he has done all that is humanly possible, just as Anton and Annie told him several chapters ago. So he surrenders and purposes in his heart to trust God to do what He knows how to do best and according to what pleases Him.

Surrendering to God is not a simple task and we can see that in Genesis 22. Abraham trusted God and He surrendered all he had to God—including his son —his only son and only child. Isaac

> I have learnt that there are some things I can't change because I'm not God

was the child God promised to give Abraham, the child he waited for for several years and, of course, the child he loved very much. But even though it didn't make sense, Abraham obeyed because He had put God first above himself and above all that he had.

Beloved one, when the act of surrender comes with tough choices, be confident enough to still choose God. Always choose God. You might look crazy to the world and you might not always understand. But God is God, and He knows what He is doing. Trust in His good and perfect will. Trust in His providence. He loves you.

# Journaling Prompt

*Have you been struggling to surrender to God? Tell Him about it.*

---

**Prayer:**
Dear Jesus, give me the courage to surrender to You.

**Today's affirmation:**
God will always be God. I surrender all to Him.

# CHAPTER 32

## *Scripture: Psalm 46:1-11*

In this chapter, Teeyana takes the first step in asking all the questions she has been scared of. She starts with Kevin because he is neutral and she knows he won't take sides. Kevin explains that it's okay to be vulnerable with God because when our hearts are in that posture, then we can realize we need him. Up to this point, Teeyana has seen weakness as a bad thing. She doesn't let others know she is struggling and certainly doesn't let others see how vulnerable she is.

But Kevin reminds her that God is not looking for people who are strong. If he was, then we wouldn't need him. He wants us to rely on Him.

> **God is not looking for people who are strong.**

In Psalm 46, the psalmist celebrates the fact that God is our refuge and our strength—an ever present help in times of trouble. This means that it doesn't matter what situation we find ourselves in, God is ever ready to be there for us. This psalm celebrates the beauty of God's strength and power, reminding us that nothing can stand in His way. We cannot compare His strength with anyone else's. It is this same God who is calling us to rely on Him.

Beloved one, true victory doesn't come from looking within yourself. It comes from total reliance on God's strength to help you overcome life's difficult situations. So come to Him today. Be vulnerable in His presence. He will strengthen your heart and help you overcome that trial. He loves you.

## Journaling Prompt

*Are you struggling to rely on God's strength?  
Tell Him about it.*

_____
_____
_____
_____
_____
_____
_____
_____
_____
_____
_____
_____
_____
_____
_____
_____
_____
_____

**Prayer:**  
Dear Jesus, help me to draw strength from Your presence.

**Today's affirmation:**  
God is my strength. I will stay in His presence always

# CHAPTER 33

### *Scripture: Exodus 14:10-25*

In this chapter, Teeyana moves on in her quest to find answers and she tackles her parents next. She starts with her mum first, who encourages her to understand that the storms of life are inevitable. Storms are something that we all go through, but the difference with us is that we serve a God who is so much bigger than the storm.

When the Israelites left Egypt after hundreds of years of slavery, they were happy because their freedom had finally come. But when they looked back and saw that the Egyptian army was pursuing them, they became terrified as they thought they  were going to die. They complained to Moses and his response was to cry out to the Lord and ask him to deliver them.

Moses believed God was bigger than their adversary, so he encouraged the Israelites to not be afraid, to stand firm and see for themselves how big God is. In His powerful nature, God showed Himself strong in that He parted the Red Sea before their very eyes. They walked through on dry land without the Egyptians hurting any of them.

Beloved one, as you go through today, remember that the God of Moses is the same God we worship today. He is able to do these things and so much more. So when you reach a storm in front of you, be confident, like Moses, to tell it how big your God is. He loves you.

# Journaling Prompt

*Are you facing a storm right now?*
*Tell that storm how big your God is.*

___

___

___

___

___

___

___

___

___

___

___

___

___

___

___

___

___

___

___

**Prayer:**
Dear Jesus, help me to always look to You when I face storms.

**Today's affirmation:**
God is bigger than any storm I face.

# CHAPTER 34

## *Scripture: Ephesians 2:1-9*

In this chapter, Teeyana speaks with her granddad and she takes her time to ask her final questions. One thing she struggles with is when her grandpa says he was okay with the fact that God didn't always give him an answer when he prayed. His response to her is simple—God owes us nothing and we are not entitled to anything from Him. But He chose to love us and sacrifice His own son for us because He is merciful and kind.

It can be very easy to feel entitled when it comes to God's good gifts. But this kind of heart posture breeds pride and we all know that God resists the proud. When we approach God's throne of grace, we need to do so knowing that we are who we are only by His grace. We didn't earn His grace. We didn't work for it and we sure don't deserve it. If God was to give us what we rightfully deserve, then we wouldn't be worthy to stand before His presence.

> **We are not entitled to anything in this life. Instead we owe Him everything.**

Instead, God created a plan to make us righteous, holy and blameless before Him because of the sacrifice of Jesus Christ. So now we have access to all His eternal riches and He makes our souls prosper because He has adopted us into His family. That is fantastic news and one we should not take for granted.

So, beloved one, instead of holding on to pride when you approach God's throne today, throw that away and assume a humble posture instead. God always gives grace to the humble. He loves you.

## Journaling Prompt

*In what ways has God's grace come through for you?*

**Prayer:**
Dear Jesus, please help me to never to take your grace for granted.

**Today's affirmation:**
God is gracious to me. His kindness and mercies never cease.

# CHAPTER 35

### *Scripture: Galatians 5:13-26*

In this chapter, we see Teeyana having another heart to heart talk with her mom, where she cautions Teeyana about how pain can make people do things they don't mean. This gives Teeyana an opportunity to reflect on the argument she had with Jayden and how she lets her pain control her words and her actions. Through reflecting on this, she realizes she was at fault and needed to apologize for the way she treated Jayden.

Sometimes we allow our emotions to control our actions so much that we forget to show grace to our neighbor. When we allow ourselves to be ruled by our emotions rather than the fruits of the spirit, the consequences are always unpleasant.

Of course, this is not something that we can do on our own. Our human nature always wants to let emotions take over. That's what the flesh does. But as children of God, we live by the spirit who helps us bear fruits even when we are struggling and dealing with pain and hurt.

So, beloved one, as you go through today, ask God to help you not to let your emotions take over your actions. But no matter what comes your way, you will still joyfully produce the fruits of the spirit. He loves you.

# Journaling Prompt

*Have your feelings ever been an obstacle to you bearing the fruits of the spirit?*

_____
_____
_____
_____
_____
_____
_____
_____
_____
_____
_____
_____
_____
_____
_____

**Prayer:**
Dear Jesus, help me not to let pain and hurt control me.

**Today's affirmation:**
I am a child of God. I will always live by the spirit.

# CHAPTER 36

## *Scripture: 2 Corinthians 12:1-10*

In this chapter, we see Jayden finally opening up to Teeyana about his past. He shares about his brother Tyler, his struggles with mental illness, and how far God has brought him on his faith and healing journey. At the beginning of this book, Jayden could barely speak about Tyler without breaking down. But now, we see him working through his emotions and keeping God at the center of the process.

Jayden shares his testimony without leaving God out of it because he knows he would never have overcome his mental health struggles without God's help. One thing he points out is that God's grace has always been sufficient for him, no matter how painful his journey is.

His grace is sufficient, no matter what the thorn in my flesh is.

Apostle Paul talks about the sufficiency of God's grace too in his second letter to the Corinthian church. He mentions in this letter that he had a thorn in his flesh to keep him from getting proud. When he cried out to God to take this thorn away, the response he got was that God's grace would be sufficient and God's power shines through in his weakness. Apostle Paul's attitude toward this response was amazing. While a lot of us would hate to have weaknesses, he proclaims here that he boasts about his weaknesses openly because, through them, others can see God's power.

Beloved one, God's grace is always sufficient, no matter how painful your situation is. His grace remains sufficient to hold you, to keep your head high, to encourage you, and to shine His power through you. Your weaknesses are testimonies of God's power because when you are weak, He is strong. He loves you.

# Journaling Prompt

*In what way has God's grace been sufficient for you?*

---

**Prayer:**
Dear Jesus, please help me to boast in my weaknesses and let Your power rest on me.

**Today's affirmation:**
God's grace will always be sufficient for me. He is my strength.

# CHAPTER 37

## *Scripture: Esther 4:1-17*

In this chapter, Teeyana goes back to college after a long weekend of confronting her fears and surrendering her life to God. Even though she has now decided to trust God, she is still scared about the situations she can't control. So she prepares to avoid any confrontations with Heather, but God has other plans for her. She hears Heather crying and when she tries to help, Heather pushes her away. But Teeyana hears God speak to her for the first time, encouraging her to talk to Heather. Naturally, as the human she is, she refuses to do this at first, but later yields to the Holy Spirit and God uses her to encourage Heather through a difficult time.

Could it be that all this happened for this very moment?

In the book of Esther—the young queen who married King Xerxes—was chosen by God to deliver the Jews. But Esther had no idea why God had allowed her to be chosen or why she was at the palace. Her uncle, Mordecai, pointed out that perhaps God had put her in the palace, so He could use her to bring salvation for her people.

Beloved one, as you go through life, you won't always see the bigger picture, but God does because He knows the end from the beginning. God might place you in situations to witness to others, but you may not realize it until the right time comes. Be ready, stay alert and continue to let your light shine no matter where you are. God is always intentional about where He places you. He loves you.

## Journaling Prompt

*Has God ever provided an opportunity for you to witness to others?*

_____
_____
_____
_____
_____
_____
_____
_____
_____
_____
_____
_____
_____
_____
_____
_____
_____
_____

**Prayer:**
Dear Jesus, please help me to recognize moments where I can be a blessing to others.

**Today's affirmation:**
I will be a blessing to others. Others will see Jesus in me.

# CHAPTER 38

*Scripture: Genesis 24:1-27*

In this chapter, we see the romance between Teeyana and Jayden going up a notch when he finally asks her to be his girlfriend. Even though Teeyana had been waiting for Jayden to ask her out from the time they met, Jayden had his reasons for waiting. He wanted to make sure Teeyana was in a good place spiritually, and he also wanted to make sure it was what God wanted him to do. Throughout the book, we have seen Jayden show his love and respect for Teeyana. He tells her the reason he waited was because he didn't want to waste her time and he wanted to be intentional from the beginning.

In Genesis chapter 24, we see that when it was time for Abraham to find a wife for his son—Isaac—he was also intentional about finding a woman who knew God. He sent his servant back to his homeland to find Isaac a wife. Throughout the story, the servant was also very intentional about seeking directions from God before making a move. Even when he met Rebecca at the well, he asked God for a sign to prove that she was the one He wanted to be Isaac's wife.

Just as our good God is intentional about us, we, too, should be intentional about our relationship with Him and our relationships with others. Being around people who know the Lord is a blessing, as you can encourage each other in your walk. It takes intentionality to form these relationships, and that starts now.

So, beloved one, as you step out today, I implore you to be intentional about forming Christ-centered relationships, because relationships built on Jesus can never be shaken. He loves you.

## Journaling Prompt

*Are you struggling to be intentional in your relationships? Tell God about it.*

___

**Prayer:**
Dear Jesus, help me to be intentional about my relationships

**Today's affirmation:**
I will be intentional about making Christ-centered relationships

# CHAPTER 39

## *Scripture: Colossians 3:1-17*

In this chapter, we see Teeyana embracing new changes in her life and one way in which she does this is by cutting her hair. She has been growing out her natural curls for a long time and she lets Amara cut off the straggly ends so she can embrace the beauty of her curls underneath. Although this act might look insignificant to some, it is a big deal for Teeyana as it represents what God is doing in her life. She admits she has been holding on to fear and doubts. But God came in with His pair of scissors and cut them all away. She is no longer the same girl she used to be, and she is embracing the new season God has her in.

**I needed to let go and let God cut away all my fears.**

This feeling of getting a new life is what we experience as believers when we come to Christ. God opens our eyes to see the treasure we have in Him. Our hearts no longer desire the things of the world and we have a new desire to serve God and live for Him all the days of our life. When we are in Him, we are His chosen people, no longer bound to sin, but free to live the life God has called us to live.

So, beloved one, as you go through today, ask God to help you embrace the new season He has you on. Ask Him to help you live out the life He has called you to live with boldness, courage and joy because you are His child. He loves you.

# Journaling Prompt

*Is God transitioning you into a new season?*
*How are you embracing the changes?*

_____
_____
_____
_____
_____
_____
_____
_____
_____
_____
_____
_____
_____
_____
_____
_____
_____

**Prayer:**
Dear Jesus, help me to let go of fear and embrace the person You want me to be.

**Today's affirmation:**
I will let go and let God mold me into who He wants me to be.

# CHAPTER 40

### *Scripture: Isaiah 53:1-12*

In this chapter, we see Jayden meeting Teeyana's parents and having a heart to heart talk with Teeyana's dad. Jayden was nervous about this meeting because he wants Mr. Sparks to like him. But in the end, he chooses to be himself and to share his story as honestly as possible. Mr. Sparks, who is understandably protective of his daughter, asks Jayden some important questions about his intentions. Jayden answers the questions with grace and finally shares about his faith journey and his brother—Tyler. This conversation helps Jayden to admit his weakness of wanting to hide his pain so he can encourage others. Mr. Sparks uses this opportunity to encourage Jayden to see that we're all broken and need a Savior.

At some stage in our lives, we will all need encouragement. Even the encourager needs to be encouraged too. The best encourager is our Lord and Savior Jesus Christ. Not only did He come to earth to walk with his creation, but He also went through great suffering for our sake. He understands what it is like to endure suffering because He did that on the cross of Calvary. But His suffering was not in vain because now we have peace, joy, comfort and, most importantly, we have healing. His body was broken for us and resurrected to new life.

So, beloved one, as you go through today, meditate on the finished work of Christ on the cross and how much peace and joy His resurrection brought you. It's okay that sometimes you need to be encouraged. God is ever ready to encourage and provide healing for your heart. He loves you.

## Journaling Prompt

*In what ways has God encouraged you recently?*

_____
_____
_____
_____
_____
_____
_____
_____
_____
_____
_____
_____
_____
_____
_____
_____

**Prayer:**
Dear Jesus, thank You for saving me and for being my greatest encourager.

**Today's affirmation:**
Jesus is my Saviour. He is my greatest encourager.

# CHAPTER 41

### *Scripture: 1 Thessalonians 5:15-18*

In this final chapter of the book, we see Teeyana living in her new season and embracing the peace God has given her. She is able to speak about her grandmother in such a way that shows she is also at peace with the whole situation. We also meet Rupert again who informs Teeyana that he lost his wife, Marjorie, and he would leave for England soon. The two are able to relate to each other's pain and as they share their thoughts with each other, Teeyana learns something valuable from the old man's words of wisdom. Rupert says that he will continue to give thanks to God.

**In every circumstance, good or bad, I'll give thanks to my God.**

When we go through trials, gratitude isn't always the first thing that comes to our minds. In our human nature, we would first want to complain, then rant, and then maybe let the whole know about how unfair it is for us to be in that situation. Not everyone will find it easy to thank God for being in a situation that is not ideal. But in the Apostle Paul's second letter to the Thessalonian church, he urged them to always be thankful for every circumstance—whether good or bad—because God is worthy of our praise and He deserves it all.

So, beloved one, as you step out today, pray that God will enable you to remain joyful, to remain prayerful and to remain grateful no matter what comes your way. He loves you.

## Journaling Prompt

*What are some of the things you are grateful to God for?*

_____
_____
_____
_____
_____
_____
_____
_____
_____
_____
_____
_____
_____
_____
_____
_____
_____

**Prayer:**
Dear Jesus, help me to always remain joyful, prayerful and grateful.

**Today's affirmation:**
I will give thanks to my God no matter what my circumstance is.

# EPILOGUE

### *Scripture: Isaiah 55:8-9*

In this epilogue, two years have passed and as Teeyana and Jayden reflect on their faith journeys, she realizes she had the wrong motives for wanting to work at Google. It was all about her and what she wanted to do. So she takes a step back to pursue something she believes will make her feel more satisfied in God. Their conversation helps them to appreciate the fact that God is sovereign. His plan is always working, even when we think it is not.

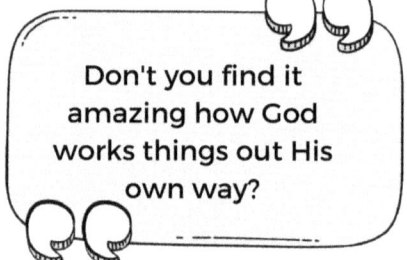

Don't you find it amazing how God works things out His own way?

When Jesus died on the cross of Calvary, it was a sad day for His disciples. They thought all hope was lost because their Savior was gone. They didn't know that Jesus' death was part of God's plan all along. Even in that moment, when it felt like there was no way out, God had a plan to do that for the sake of our salvation. In His sovereignty, He doesn't think the same way we do, and He doesn't work the same way we do. But one thing we can be comforted about is that He knows the plans He has for us, He knows the way that we take, and His thoughts toward us are always good and perfect.

So, beloved heart, as you step out today, rest in the knowledge of God's sovereignty. He knows your past, present and future. As long as God is involved, all will be well, because victory belongs to Him. He loves you.

# Journaling Prompt

*Can you think about scenarios where you realized God's plans were better than yours?*

_____
_____
_____
_____
_____
_____
_____
_____
_____
_____
_____
_____
_____
_____
_____
_____

**Prayer:**
Dear Jesus, thank You for Your good and perfect thoughts towards me.

**Today's affirmation:**
God knows it all. His plans are always perfect. I will forever trust Him.

# A CALL TO SURRENDER

If you're reading this and you're yet to surrender your life to Jesus Christ as your Lord and Saviour, here's an open invitation to do so today. It is not too late. The Lord's open arms are waiting, and He is calling you to come home. There's no pain He can't heal. Jesus has already paid the price for you. He wants you to abandon your pride today and run to Him. He has loved you from the beginning of time and He always will. If you want to take that bold step today, please say this prayer with me;

*Dear Jesus, I come before you today with thanksgiving in my heart. I accept that you are God and I am not. I am a sinner, but You alone are the Forgiver of sins. Please come into my heart today. I surrender my all to you as my Lord and Saviour. Make me clean and teach me how to love and obey you. In Jesus' name I've prayed. Amen.*

If you've prayed this prayer of faith and are willing to walk into your new life with Jesus, congratulations. Welcome to God's family. Please get plugged into a local church if you haven't already done so. Commit to studying the Bible with fellow believers and find a spiritual mentor you trust who will help you along the journey. If you would like to share a testimony with me, please reach out to me on social media or using the contact form found on my website: www.joanembola.co.uk.

Until the next book,
Lots of love,
Joan 💕

# A Plea

Thank you so much for reading this book. I would be very grateful if you could please leave a review online. Reviews are very important because they help the book become more visible to others so they can be blessed by it too. Thank you again and God bless you.

## A Free Short Story

Subscribe to my free monthly newsletter to stay up to date with book news and to also get a free short story called A Promise To Keep, which follows a Nigerian couple—Dayo and Dara as they navigate the challenges of life while learning about endurance and what it means to experience the goodness of God.

## About The Author

Joan Embola is a UK-based Cameroonian-Nigerian Christian author who aims to share God's love one word at a time. She writes books about diverse characters whose hope-filled stories point to the love and goodness of God in our broken world. She is a qualified Physician Associate and also the founder of Love Qualified, a ministry dedicated to encouraging others to experience the sovereign love of the one true God who has qualified us to be His beloved ones. She is a passionate lover and teacher of God's Word, as shared on her YouTube channel, blog, and podcast. When she's not writing or curled up with a book, you'll find her watching movies, YouTube videos, or making memories with her family and friends.

You can connect with her at [www.joanembola.co.uk](www.joanembola.co.uk) and on Instagram, YouTube and her podcast. Subscribe to her newsletter to stay up to date with more book news, cover reveals, how to sign up for advanced reader copies, and fun giveaways.

www.ingramcontent.com/pod-product-compliance
Lightning Source LLC
Chambersburg PA
CBHW042118100526
44587CB00025B/4111